Studies *in* Personality, Social *and* Clinical Psychology

Studies *in* Personality, Social *and* Clinical Psychology

Nonobvious Findings

RUSSELL EISENMAN

Lanham • New York • London

University Press of America,® Inc.
4720 Boston Way
Lanham, Maryland 20706

3 Henrietta Street
London WC2E 8LU England

Printed in the United States of America
British Cataloging in Publication Information Available

ISBN 0–8191–9674–6

The paper used in this publication meets the minimum requirements of American National Standard for Information Sciences—Permanence of Paper for Printed Library Materials, ANSI Z39.48–1984.

Dedication

This book is dedicated to my family:

my mother Georgia, brother Bob, daughter Susan, son David, niece Jenny, and my daughter's two cats Maxwell and Thimble (who, along with my daughter, live with me). Also, it is dedicated to the memory of my father Abram.

Table of Contents

Preface

This book reports investigations where nonobvious findings emerged in a variety of studies in the personality, social, or clinical psychology areas. Due to the hindsight bias, many will claim, after reading the chapters, "Oh, I would have known that." But, my guess is that they would not have anticipated the findings, at least not in most cases.

I found it really amazing that, for example, most felons convicted in state courts serve little or no prison time; little education about sex occurred in the AIDS education classes studied; a prison treatment program put barriers in the way of treatment due to staff opposition; and that psychoanalysis and feminism have both betrayed their earlier radical roots and have become, to some extent, oppressive. These are just some of the examples of nonobvious findings which emerged from my studies. Some of the studies are statistical while others involved my personal observations and are thus more informal. But, all, in my opinion, have yielded important findings.

I am most grateful to all who have helped me. A big thanks for all of you out there. Special thanks to Linda Brannon who provided expert computer and printing help, and Patrick Moreno who critiqued this preface and helped improve it.

I would appreciate your feedback. What do you think? Write to me:

Russell Eisenman, Ph.D.
Department of Psychology
McNeese State University
Lake Charles, LA 70609-1895

Chapter 1

Juvenile Delinquency

Important articles and books have been written that provide insight into juvenile delinquents (Agee, 1979; Alexander & Parsons, 1982; Bennett, 1981; Blaske, Borduin, Henggeler, & Mann, 1989; Eisenman, 1991, 1994; Goldstein, 1990; Goldstein & Keller, 1987; Klingsporn, Force, & Burdsal, 1990; Mathias, DeMuro, & Allison, 1984; Morris & Braukmann, 1987; Rivers, 1987; Quay, 1965, 1987; Weissman, 1991). The purpose of the present article is to give an overview into what is defined as "juvenile delinquent" and discuss some of the important issues. We need this kind of understanding, along with treatment techniques, if we are going to work effectively with this population of offenders. Many of the insights in this article are based on my having worked for close to two years in a prison treatment program for youthful offenders, doing individual and group psychotherapy, diagnostic assessments, writing parole board reports, and directing the substance abuse program.

Definition and Understanding

What is a juvenile delinquent? There are two basic definitions: (1) crime or (2) status offenses by a person defined as not yet being an adult. The legal age of adulthood varies from state to state, but is usually 17 or 18. A crime is anything that the laws of the state define as illegal. Status offenses are things that the state holds the youth responsible for, although these things would not be illegal if the person were an adult. Examples include not attending school, staying out too late at night, or defiance of parents. A juvenile can actually be sent to a juvenile prison for a status offense violation, although they are typically put on probation in custody of their parents, and threatened by the court with more dire consequences (incarceration) if they are disobedient. Status offenders have been seen as precriminal. The idea is that they are on the road to crime if they are not turned around and made to be more conforming. However, the concept of status offense is a controversial one, since the youth has not done anything criminal, and many question controlling them with the powers of the state and the threat of imprisonment. For most people, when they hear the term "juvenile delinquent," they think of the criminal and not of the status offender. There is also concern that, at times, girls may be seen as status offenders more readily than boys, due to society's having stricter and more confining standards for females. Those concerned with this say that it reflects prejudice against females, since society imposes a stricter standard of conformity on females than on males.

Although we have historically thought of juveniles as innocent kids, much horrible crime is committed by juvenile delinquents. They can do just as much violence or theft as adults, but our concept is that they deserve more sympathy since they are still forming, and thus should not be held totally responsible for their behavior. And, when they are held accountable, often they receive a much lesser sentence than an adult would. However, in recent times, this problem has been addressed by some courts having the right to certify juveniles as adults, for the sake of trial, and thus they are tried as adults and suffer adult penalties. In effect, they have legally lost their juvenile status as far as the trial is concerned. However, even if convicted they may be sent to juvenile rather than adult facilities. When juveniles are sent to adult prisons, they have often been raped and exploited by some of the adult prisoners.

Dysfunctional families are often found when the background of juvenile delinquents are investigated. The delinquent typically comes from a poverty background with either an absent father or a father who is cold and physically punitive. Or, the mother may be a drug user and unable to cope with being a parent. These findings are more likely to occur for lower socioeconomic status youth who are delinquent, but sometimes occur with middle and upper-class youth, too. Incidentally, the vast majority of juvenile delinquents in prison are from lower-class backgrounds. Either lower-class youth commit most of the crimes, or the system prosecutes and imprisons them but not higher status youth.

Youth who murder often have been rather seriously physically and psychologically abused by their parents. As a result of beatings or other physical trauma, many murderers have brain damage, although this is often not known or ignored. The youth do not want to admit to being deformed and thus conceal their brain damage or mental retardation, even though it might help get them a lesser sentence. And, the parents are either ignorant or not willing to talk about their child's problems because they are responsible for beatings, using drugs while pregnant, and so forth.

Background of Abuse

Juvenile delinquents have often suffered physical, sexual, or psychological abuse when growing up. The victimizer may be a parent, a relative, or a stranger. Due to their rage or confusion as a result of the abuse, committing crimes often follows. Either the juvenile is angry at the abuse and powerlessness, and acts out by doing anti-social things, or they learn from their victimizer and do the same things to others. This doing the same to others is especially the case for juvenile sex offenders, who often first were victims themselves. Now, they victimize others. The good news is that most abused children do not go on to abuse others, but a substantial percentage do. Early intervention with parents may help prevent crimes from ever happening, by preventing the abuse before it occurs. Many parents abuse their children because the parents are immature, confused, or under stress. Many parents are not equipped to be parents, and treat their children with abuse or indifference.

Anti-social Parents

There is another way in which parents help their children to become criminals. There may be little or no physical, sexual, or psychological abuse leading to juvenile delinquency, but the parents are, themselves, anti-social. Thus, in a sense the child grows up following normal rules of socialization, but in these cases the child is socialized to an anti-social standard. The parents may be criminals, or they may violate certain laws, often in a flagrant fashion, such as by using drugs in their child's presence. The child learns that this is the normal, approved way within his or her household, and adapts the parents values. Thus, the road is set for the child to become a juvenile delinquent. For example, one of the prisoners I worked with, in a prison treatment program for youthful offenders, was born into a family in which the parents were members of an anti-social motorcycle gang. To him, crime was the normal way of life. He was simply following the rules laid down by his parents, just as most kids do. But, whereas the rules of most parents call for conformity to social norms, the rules of his parents called for defiance.

Social Class

When we think of crime we usually think of lower-class people, and indeed our prisons are primarily filled with lower socioeconomic class people, including many minorities. But the middle or upper class youth may also be delinquent, but perhaps avoids going to prison, either through preferential treatment, having better attorneys, etc. It would be interesting to study more the family background of middle and upper class delinquents. The little work that has been done in this area suggests that they may also suffer from such things as neglect, unconcerned parents, etc.

Free Will?

A totally different view of crime from the one we have presented thus far puts the blame squarely on the shoulders of the offender. According to this view, people have free will and commit crimes because they choose to do so. They are not seen as victims of family background, but as bad people who do bad things. A slightly modified version of this approach would be that there is something in the offender which predisposes him or her toward committing crimes. This could possibly be brain chemistry which makes the person oriented toward thrill seeking. Perhaps some people have such a strong need for sensation seeking that ordinary excitements do not satisfy them, and under the right circumstances, such as a group which encourages them, they will commit crimes. Yet another view which places the responsibility primarily on the individual would be approaches which suggest that many criminals suffer from brain damage or other physical problems which interfere with good judgment. All these explanations have in common that they focus on the individual as being responsible and shy away from seeing the social setting, including the family, as having much to do with the juvenile becoming delinquent. It should be pointed out that an attempt to explain crime by saying that many criminals possess an extra Y chromosome, thus putting the cause squarely on a genetic basis, has been shown to be inadequate. Most criminals do not possess an extra Y chromosome, and those who do seem to have low intelligence and are not made to be criminals by their chromosomal abnormality. However, it could be that in the future research will find some chromosomal basis of criminality. Perhaps something in the individual will be discovered which makes the person predisposed toward criminal behavior. But, we do not have such evidence at this point in time.

Applications

Given that we think of some juveniles as delinquent, there are two obvious applications we can make. One, we need some way of controlling those juveniles who disobey the law. Here we have the whole criminal justice system: police, juvenile courts, probation officers, prisons, etc. Second, we can try to help the juvenile via treatment. While some would say that prison or probation is treatment, what I have in mind here is some kind of intervention that a social worker, psychologist, or psychiatrist might make.

There are three kinds of prevention. Primary prevention occurs when we prevent something bad from happening before the person shows any signs of a problem. Drug education in the early school grades would be an example. Secondary prevention occurs when we work with an at-risk population. For example, helping a youth who lives in a high crime area where drugs are sold and laws are often violated, but who himself is not delinquent, would be secondary prevention. He is at risk for becoming a delinquent, given his environment, but he has not become delinquent yet. Tertiary prevention occurs when the problem has already occurred and then we do something. Treating a disease after the person has become sick is tertiary prevention. So is doing psychotherapy with people who already are mentally ill, or doing some kind of intervention with someone who is already a delinquent. Unfortunately, most of society's preventive attempts are tertiary prevention, whereas primary prevention would seem to be the most effective, followed by secondary prevention. Psychologists and psychiatrists are typically called upon for tertiary prevention.

Likewise social workers, but some of the time they may intervene in a primary or secondary fashion, as when they do home visits and assess the problems in a home and devise some strategy for improving things. Psychologists and psychiatrists could, of course, do primary and secondary prevention, and sometimes they do, especially if they work with some agency, such as a school, and try to prevent problems before they occur. From working in a prison treatment program for youthful offenders (which is tertiary prevention) I have come to believe that it may be too late to change most of the juvenile delinquents once they become, say, 16 years old. Primary or secondary preventive efforts would seem the intelligent way to go. By the time an offender is 16 years old he or she may have a long history of crime and may be dedicated to their anti-social lifestyle. Of course, some 16 year olds can be helped, especially if they are fairly new to crime. Many juvenile delinquents have no sense of how they could be other than a criminal. Thus, treatment efforts need to provide them with alternatives and with skills, such as education or job training, to meet these alternatives.

Treating Juveniles Differently

Should juveniles be treated differently than adults? Most people would say "yes," at least most of the time. But, the idea that juveniles should be treated differently than adults is a fairly modern idea. For example, in the middle ages people had no conception of childhood, and their art often shows babies who look like small adults. Until quite recently, juveniles were often placed in prison with adults, where they were sometimes subject to rape or other abuse. Some states still place juveniles in adult prisons.

Thinking of someone as a juvenile delinquent, instead of simply as a delinquent (criminal), often means that the juvenile receives what are supposed to be special considerations. For example, the juvenile may not be "convicted of a crime" but instead has "a sustained petition" declaring him or her delinquent. The penalties may be much less than if an adult had committed the crime.

Since juveniles are being treated differently, it used to be held that the juvenile court was not really a court in the adult sense, but a place where the judge was there to help the youth. One consequence of this thinking was that the adult right to have an attorney, even if one could not afford one, was not granted to juveniles. Thus, those charged with juvenile delinquency would face the possibility of being convicted and sent to prison, but might not have a lawyer during their trial. The United States Supreme Court changed that in 1967 in a case known as In re Gault, in which they ruled that juveniles are entitled to adult-like protections, including having an attorney. No more would juveniles be tried and convicted without legal counsel.

It was previously said that juveniles may receive lesser penalties for crimes than adults. Sometimes the penalties are worse. The two examples are 1. in status offenses, wherein the offense, such as disobeying parents, would not even be a crime if the juvenile were an adult and 2. in instances where the juvenile may be confined in a juvenile prison until he becomes an adult. Thus, for example 2, an adult who breaks into a warehouse may receive a three year sentence, while a 14-year old may be confined until he is 18, or perhaps even until he is 21-years old. In this case, the person would have received a shorter sentence had he been an adult. The use of status offense as a basis for charging or imprisoning juveniles has received much criticism from social scientists as unfair. However, those who favor retaining it see it as an effective social control mechanism for what they consider criminal tendencies.

Another concern is sentencing disparity. A youth in one jurisdiction may be sent to prison for his offense, while had he been in another city he would have received probation. Different communities have different standards, so justice will not be equal across all jurisdictions. Yet a third option, often used with juveniles, is restitution. Here the offender may have to re-pay what he has stolen, possibly by having a certain amount deducted each month from his wages, if he has a job.

Sex Differences

As with adults, most juvenile delinquents are male. Females comprise a much smaller percentage of offenders. However, the crime rate among females is increasing. Why this should be the case is not clear. Some have said that the feminist movement, which advocates greater freedom from traditional roles for women, is to blame, but others say this argument is without merit. If females have greater opportunities for crime, such as opportunities to embezzle by being employed vs. their mother who stayed at home, it would seem that opportunity would at least partially account for the greater incidence of female crime. Alternatively, it could be that society today focuses more on arresting females, e. g., for drug possession or sale. There are data from the U. S. Department of Justice which supports this second view about arrests of females for drugs. However, both the feminist and drug arrest explanations could be correct. Each might independently contribute to the recent increase in arrests and imprisonment of females. Whatever the answer, the vast majority of juvenile or adult crime is committed by males.

Solutions?

Solving the problem of crime, juvenile or adult, is not easy. Several interventions show at least some promise, as supported by research studies or case histories. First, locking up juveniles for a long time at least prevents them from doing anything while they are imprisoned. This approach is known as incapacitation, and is especially favored by those who have little or no faith in psychotherapy treatment as a way to reduce crime. Second, diversion programs which do something other than put the juvenile in detention sometimes show benefit. Here, the youth is sent to something other than secure confinement, such as a probation program which may have activities for the youth, or which may demand restitution as part of the probation. Third, success can sometimes occur via psychotherapy, especially if a good therapist can tap into what the real problems are <u>and</u> get the juvenile to work on these issues. Fourth, and best, a multifaceted approach seems to work best, in which many of the first three methods are used, along with intervention which helps the juvenile find work, succeed in school, get closer with his parents, etc. This last approach involves tackling many possible avenues, and has shown the most effectiveness in reducing recidivism. This makes sense, since juvenile delinquents typically have many problems, ranging from estrangement from their family to poor school skills.

None of the above solutions are easy. The juvenile delinquent may be the victim of poverty, abuse, low intelligence, anti-social friends, etc. The more one can intervene to deal with a wide array of these problems, the better the chance for turning the juvenile delinquent into either (a) a noncriminal or (b) one who is still a criminal but less of a menace to society, e. g., a burglar instead of a murderer. Although people usually do not think of (b) or see it as a failure (the person is still a criminal) it is actually an important achievement and often all that can be hoped for in youths strongly committed to crime as their way of life. Any kind of victory, however small, is better than leaving these youths to continue in the direction they were headed before intervention.

References

Agee, V. L. (1979). *Treatment of the violent incorrigible adolescent.* Lexington, MA: Lexington Books.

Alexander, J. F. & Parsons, B. V. (1982). Short-term behavioral intervention with delinquent families: Impact on family process and recidivism. *Journal of Abnormal Psychology, 81,* 219-225.

Bennett, J. (1981). *Oral history and delinquency: The rhetoric of criminology.* Chicago: University of Chicago Press.

Blaske, D. M., Borduin, C. M., Henggeler, S. W., & Mann, B. J. (1989). Individual, family, and peer characteristics of adolescent sex offenders and assaultive offenders. *Developmental Psychology, 25,* 846-855.

Eisenman, R. (1991). *From crime to creativity: Psychological and social factors in deviance.* Dubuque, IA: Kendall/Hunt.

Eisenman, R. (1994). *Contemporary social issues: Drugs, crime, creativity and education.* Ashland, OH: BookMasters.

Goldstein, A. P. (1990). *Delinquents on delinquency.* Champaign, IL: Research Press.

Goldstein, A. P., & Keller, H. (1987). *Aggressive behavior: Assessment and intervention.* New York: Pergamon.

Klingsporn, M. J., Force, R. C., & Burdsal, C. (1990). The effectiveness of various degrees and circumstances of program completion of young male offenders in a residential treatment center. *Journal of Clinical Psychology, 46,* 491-500.

Methias, R. A., DeMuro, P., & Allison, R. S. (Eds.). (1984). *Violent juvenile offenders.* San Francisco: National Council on Crime and Delinquency.

Morris, E. K., & Braukmann, C. J. (1987). *Behavioral approaches to crime and delinquency.* New York: Plenum.

Rivers, P. C. (Ed.). (1987). *Alcohol and addictive behaviors.* Lincoln, NE: University of Nebraska Press.

Quay, H. C. (1965). Psychopathic personality as pathological stimulation-seeking. *American Journal of Psychiatry, 122*,180-183.

Quay, H. C. (Ed.). (1987). *Handbook of juvenile delinquency.* New York: Wiley.

Weissman, H. N. (1991). Forensic psychological examination of the child witness in cases of alleged sexual abuse. *American Journal of Orthopsychiatry, 61*, 48-58.

Questions

1. What were the major points in this chapter? Use the rest of the page for your answer.

Questions

2. What are your opinions about the findings of this chapter? Use the rest of the page for your answer.

Chapter 2

Realities of the Criminal Justice System

The criminal justice system often functions very differently than many people would think. The police beating of Rodney King in Los Angeles was videotaped, and many people got to see what can happen when a person is stopped by the police. In this case, King was partially to blame, as he initially resisted the police. This is no way justifies the savage beating he received, but the whole event was different than what is often portrayed in the media, even on so-called reality programming, where a camera follows the police around. In the case of reality programming, if the cameraman recorded misconduct by the police, probably it would not be shown because (a) the cameraman or production company developed a comradeship with the police and (b) if it were shown the relationship with the police, including their cooperation, might be terminated.

To Incarcerate or Not to Incarcerate: It may Depend on the State

What happens when a person is arrested may depend greatly on local circumstances. I found, in a nationwide study of disposition of juvenile offenses, that in some states a repeat offender juvenile is highly likely to be sentenced to incarceration, while other states are highly unlikely to incarcerate (Eisenman, 1991b). Thus, some states seem to have a tough, law-and-order, lock 'em up philosophy, while other states seem to be guided by concern for the age of the juvenile, and seek to avoid imprisonment. The former viewpoint may reflect the philosophy on incapacitation, whereby it is believed that even if no rehabilitation occurs, at least the offender is unable to offend while imprisoned. Thus, society is protected from him during this time. The latter viewpoint may reflect a more humanistic philosophy, whereby the juvenile is seen as capable of rehabilitation, and incarceration is seen as overly harsh or perhaps leading to further criminalization by exposing the offender to other criminals and general harsh and degrading treatment.

Do Convicted Felons Go to Prison?

Many people, no doubt, believe that when a person is convicted in a state court of a felony, he is likely to be sentenced to the state penitentiary. This notion is examined in the present report, using data from the United States Bureau of Justice Statistics, to see how true the assumption is. While the idea that a convicted felon could receive probation only may be shocking to some, it is one of the options available to courts. The data reported here do not involve people convicted in federal courts. The whole issue of sentencing is an important one, since different jurisdictions may handle the same crime differently (Benekos, 1992; Blumstein, Cohen, Martin, & Tonry, 1983; Eisenman, 1991b), which has led some to call for sentencing reforms so that similar offenses will receive similar sentences. However, imposing uniformity of sentence on judges often takes away their ability to use discretion in a helpful fashion, e. g. showing leniency to someone who seems capable of reform or imposing a necessary harsh sentence on someone deemed a great threat to the community (Goodstein & Hepburn, 1985).

The present discussion is based on Bureau of Justice Statistics data about nationwide use of sentencing by state courts for convicted felons, and is based on state court convictions of adults in 1986. In that year, a total of approximately 583,000 adult felons were convicted in state courts. The data reported here comes primarily from two surveys of 100 counties across the United States and a follow-up study of probation in 32 of the counties. Court records were used to obtain a sample of 12,370 cases representing 79,043 felons placed on probation in 32 counties in 17 states. Additional data on adult felons sentenced to incarceration come from several surveys of court records by the Bureau of Justice Statistics for the year 1986.

Outcomes: Felons Do Not Necessarily Go to Prison

Five kinds of outcomes were obtained: probation with no incarceration, probation with some jail time, probation with some prison time, jail only, or prison only. The distinction between jail and prison is that jails are usually run by city or county authorities and typically house people awaiting trial or people serving sentences which are usually for lesser offences and lesser periods of time than those sent to state prisons. Prisons are typically run by the state authorities, and house the most serious offenders.

More than half of the convicted felons received sentences which were, essentially, probation. However, many of these were required to serve brief jail or prison sentences as well as be on probation. The sentences were typically of five months or less. Specifically, 52% of convicted felons

received probation, but this was probation only for 32%. For 15% some jail time was included, while for 6% some prison time was included.

Convicted felons sentenced to jail only comprised 6%, while the disposition which many may assume is what all convicted felons receive, prison only, occurred for 40%.

Discussion

If one watches television or movies about crime, the convicted felon is typically sentenced to a long prison sentence. However, in real life, more than half receive probation, although 21% receive some brief incarceration along with their probation. But, 31% simply receive probation, with no sentence of incarceration at all. This is quite different than what the average citizen might expect from watching the media or from hearing about our wars on crime.

Prison overpopulation may account, in part, for the findings. It is easier to sentence people to prisons when there is a lot of space, but when some prisons or jails are under court order to release inmates due to overcrowding, then the hands of the court may be tied. Another reason may be that those in power may believe that not all offenders should be incarcerated. People who are first time offenders (as far as the court knows; see Eisenman 199la and 1991c for a suggestion that many crimes are undetected) may receive sympathy from the courts, especially given the overcrowding in prisons. And, people convicted of the less serious felonies, such as burglary as opposed to rape or murder, might be seen as not needing to be in prison. There is some justification for this view, in that prisons are often schools for crime, teaching offenders how to be better criminals and have greater identification with anti-social beliefs. Thus, sentencing someone to prison (or jail) is not necessarily going to make that person more likely to live a crime free life than sentencing that person to probation.

On the other hand, there are some people who will continue to be criminals and who will hurt many innocent citizens. Society would best be protected, at least while that person is locked up, if incarceration was imposed. Also, just because the person is convicted of one of the lesser felonies does not mean that the person has not committed other more serious crimes for which they have not been caught or that they will not commit more serious crimes at a later data. Burglars do not always remain burglars.

While it is not always clear what the appropriate criminal justice sanction should be for convicted felons, the present report at least shows what is being done. Far fewer convicted adult felons go to prison than many might expect. And, some go only for a few months and then are on probation. Whether or not these findings represent a desirable condition is another issue. We must first know what is happening before we can decide whether or not it should be changed.

References

Benekos, P. J. (1992). Public policy and sentencing reform: The politics of corrections. *Federal Probation, 56,* (no. 1, March), 4-10.

Blumstein, A., Cohen, J., Martins, S., & Tonry, M. (Eds.) (1983). *Research on sentencing: The search for reform.* (Vol. 1 & 2). Washington, DC: National Academy Press.

Eisenman, R. (1991a). *From crime to creativity: Psychological and social factors in deviance.* Dubuque, IA: Kendall/Hunt.

Eisenman, R. (1991b). Is justice equal?: A look at restitution, probation, or incarceration in six states. *Louisiana Journal of Counseling and Development, 11* (no. 2), 47-50.

Eisenman, R. (1991c). Monitoring and postconfinement treatment of sex offenders: An urgent need. *Psychological Reports, 69,* 1089-1090.

Goodstein, L., & Hepburn, J. (1985). *Determinate sentencing and imprisonment: A failure of reform.* Cincinnati: Anderson.

Questions

1. What were the major points in this chapter? Use the rest of the page for your answer.

Questions

2. What are your opinions about the findings of this chapter? Use the rest of the page for your answer.

Chapter 3

Warning—Working in a Prison May Be Hazardous to Your Emotional and Physical Health

For close to two years I worked as senior clinical psychologist in a prison treatment program for youthful male offenders in California. This state run program was considered a model program by many, but there were, nevertheless, many problems involved in working in such a program. People are aware that working in a prison can pose a physical danger. Not enough people are aware that there are hazards for one's emotional health as well. Not only does one face hostility and potential physical danger from anti-social prisoners, but the nontreatment staff can give a therapist a very hard time, leading to emotional problems of anger, burnout, stress, and so forth. For example, many nontreatment staff have no orientation to therapy, so even if the program is set up to provide psychotherapy, as ours was, there will be hostility from those who do not believe in it. This is true even though part of their jobs entails counseling prisoners or at least helping those of us who are doing treatment. For me, both the prisoners and the staff were sources of job stress.

The Prisoners

The prisoners in the treatment program received individual and group psychotherapy from clinical psychologists, social workers, and a psychiatrist. Although all were dedicated therapists, working with prisoners can be quite difficult. Some might think of people working at a state facility as being somehow inferior to others at more prestigious settings. However, the staff was not composed of rejects from other settings: they were, in my opinion, high quality professionals.

The prisoners were juvenile delinquents, through 17 years old, and some young adults 18 to 25 years old. The latter were ones deemed inappropriate for the state's adult prison system. Often this was because the prisoner was too weak or immature to fit in with the adults. Since we had one of the few treatment programs in the state, our prisoners had to be judged emotionally disturbed to get into the facility. The youngest prisoner in our program during my almost two years there was 14 years old, and the oldest was 28, the latter being an exception to the usual 25-year old limit. He was a weak, partially deaf, probably brain damaged child molester, who could fit into no other program in the state and who had failed parole at least twice. The model age in our facility was 16 or 18 years old (different at different times: 18 during my first year, 16 during my second).

This was a difficult group to treat successfully. Not only were they criminals, but they were seriously disturbed, with a full range of mental disorders. About one-third were psychotic. Early on I had heard reports of an 85 percent recidivism rate from prisoners in the state's three intensive treatment programs (which our treatment program was officially known as), but I tried not to think about that too much.

I wondered, how could I succeed where others had failed? In the end, the low probability of preventing a return to crime was very frustrating to me. But, the major source of stress was the way one was treated by the prisoners. These were anti-social, anti-authority youths who had built their lives on manipulating others. The treated me similarly, even though I was often kind to them. To some extent kindness was reciprocated, but usually was misinterpreted as weakness. Never had I been lied to or been the victim of attempted manipulations so often. These prisoners were real pros.

Even worse to me than the constant dishonesty and manipulations was the undercurrent of hostility. These were very angry, aggressive individuals, for the most part. With few exceptions, their orientation was one of violence to solve problems. Even though I felt safer than most people would probably think, there was such an undercurrent of violence that it had to--and did--have an effect on me. For example, I tried to make it a habit not to turn my back on the prisoners. This was often difficult, such as when I had one or more prisoners with me and was unlocking the door to the trailer where I had my office and did therapy. The habit of a lifetime is to turn your back as you face and open the door. I tried to overcome this habit.

The prisoners would often steal from each other and threaten to fight one another. Occasionally these threats became reality. It was less likely that they would attack any of the therapists, as they did see us as trying to help them. We were not making demands on their immediate behavior. In contrast, the guards had the duty of getting the prisoners to stand in line, be quiet, etc. They were subject to violent attacks, almost always, in my experience, fist fighting.

One example might serve to indicate the kind of stressful situation I constantly faced. I was working very well in therapy with a prisoner I will call Jose. He opened up to me while remaining defiant to the rest of the staff. On one occasion while in my office for individual psychotherapy, he asked to be allowed to make a phone call. It was a privilege to call from the therapist's office, as the phone on the unit only permitted collect calls. Here he would not have to make a collect call, and could phone someone who was poor and might not want to or be able to accept a collect call. He made about three calls, but never got through. After the second call I told him he could make one more but that this definitely would be the last call. It is very important to set limits and stick to them with these anti-social youth. Despite his begging, I remained firm--no more phone calls. After much complaining he said "What if I knock you out?" This seemed to be both a joke and a threat. I said. "Then you can do whatever you want"--and that put a stop to any further direct threats of a knock out. However he proceeded to talk of how he used to do amateur boxing and knew how to punch. He then punched me in the knee. I felt no pain, but did hear something pop. I said "I hope you haven't injured my knee"--to which he replied, mocking my concern, "I hope you haven't injured my knee. You sound like a girl."

Jose's viewpoint was consistent with how the prisoners thought. They were into being tough, macho guys, and any complaint about injury or pain was generally taboo. The example is little unusual since it involved direct physical contact. That was not usually the case with the therapists. More often violence was in the air, or one was subjected to hostile stares or otherwise bad vibes. Fortunately, my knee did not seem to be injured, as I never experienced any pain. The popping sound was probably that of his hand; he had apparently pulled his punch to avoid hurting me.

It should be obvious by now that I do not consider a prison a fun place to work. At first, perhaps because of the novelty, I was excited and found the job extremely interesting. It was, in fact, very educational; but, as time went on, the constant cursing, hostility, and unwillingness to change became a bit much. It is easy to have sympathy for the prisoners if you know their life histories. Most come from horrible poverty, parental abuse or neglect, and general deprivation. But, what this produces is a person who has no empathy for other victims and who sees anti-social behavior, including crime, as the way to go.

The Nontreatment Staff

It it were not bad enough facing the stress which the prisoners engendered, there was also the stress from the custodial staff. This includes those who were called "Youth Counselors" but who were basically glorified guards, and who did very little counseling. Most of the nontreatment staff were from lower-class backgrounds with limited education. Some had college degrees, often having been college athletes, such as football or basketball players. Most had no sense of mental illness or treatment. Often, some staff would un-do or hamper what the therapists were trying to do. A former professional football player, for instance, would tell me I could not do therapy with a prisoner because he was being locked up for misbehavior. Since this was a treatment program, such a position was obviously incorrect, and I could get it reversed after talking to the higher-ups. However, it was a strain to have to face repeatedly such anti-treatment sabotage. Typical reaction: in a staff meeting he once said "We had a good program until these outsiders [therapists] came here." Twice I saw him throw punches at prisoners in totally unnecessary occasions. He stayed on the job quite some time, until he was promoted to a higher status, higher paying security position within the prison system.

Aside from the frustration of trying to keep a treatment program going among people who had power but knew little about treatment, was the stress of having to put up with my supervisor. I reported directly to a supervisor--in my case a man with only a bachelor's degree in business, but lots of prison experience. I felt terrible about being reprimanded for allegedly violating some silly rule (he seemed to enjoy doing this), or about being ordered to do treatment or prepare a report in a way I felt incorrect and perhaps unethical. Here I was a Ph. D. clinical psychologist being told what to do by someone I considered unqualified to make treatment decisions. I remember once thinking "This is a high-level job, but I am made to feel like shit."

The therapy staff (and other staff) were often treated much like the prisoners. As part of my job, I had to go to three weeks of supervisor's training at the state capital, hundreds of miles away. Like most of the training I was required to attend I got almost nothing useful from it. However, I did learn of the incredible emphasis put on what was called "adverse action" against employees. this involves writing them up for infractions, when can be seen as a corrective measure per se, but which can also lead to the employee being fired, in the extreme case. During the training I almost asked the following question, but did not: "Is there so much emphasis put on adverse action because this is a prison setting and there is a spirit of fault-finding and control?" Probably, they would not have understood my question.

The Therapy Staff

I got along much better with the therapy staff. We had a similar mission, of helping the prisoners via therapy to be less criminal, and also had similar training. I got along as well with the three social workers and the one psychiatrist as I did with the two clinical psychologists I supervised. No doubt our high level of education (and intelligence?) helped us see things in roughly similar ways. Also, we were not primarily concerned with security, and that gave us some room to deal with the prisoners as fallible human beings, instead of always seeing them as potential escapees. I became close friends with the psychiatrist and with one of the clinical psychologists. However, the latter left soon after I arrived. Many therapy staff stayed for only a short while, being unwilling to put up with the kinds of things I have described. The fact that I got along so well with the psychiatrist was very helpful, since we were the two people in charge of therapy for the entire treatment program. Had we disagreed a great deal or been in political opposition to one another, it could have made effective running of the therapy programs very difficult.

There was one strange thing which happened from time to time, especially when I first arrived. I realized that some of the therapy staff would report me to my supervisor for some alleged wrong. Instead of coming to me and saying "You know, you should not allow the volunteer to be in the next room, alone, with that prisoner," they would tell my supervisor, who would then tell me. This was something I had not encountered before, at least not on a steady basis, and seemed to indicate a lack of trust among the therapists, or perhaps a way for them to curry favor at my expense. Also, on one occasion, a therapist offered to transfer a prisoner to my caseload from hers, since he seemed to like me a lot, and was not doing that well with her. I accepted, but later, in a staff meeting of everyone, custodial as well as treatment staff, she publicly accused me of stealing the patient from her. I denied this, but when one of the clinical psychologists, who had overheard her offer the patient to me, tried to speak on my behalf, he was told by my supervisor to be quiet. He was not allowed to speak. The therapist who lost the patient continued to complain about my alleged theft, until my supervisor (who was also her supervisor) told her "Put a sock in it."

These strange, hostile encounters with the therapy staff added to the hazards of working there, since it made me feel "Who can I trust?" But, fortunately, they were infrequent occurrences relative to the harsh treatment I received from prisoners, nontreatment staff, and supervisor.

Some Conclusions

The stress of working with anti-social youth and sometimes hostile staff became more that I wanted to bear, and I left the prison after less than two years. Just as the former professional football player was promoted, my supervisor received an award for being an outstanding supervisor. While a prison is a difficult place to run and I can sympathize with many of the problems, I found the work too stressful and too unrewarding. So, sandwiched between my stints in academia was this incredible experience which produced much insight and much stress. I am grateful for what I learned and for the good relationships I had with many of my colleagues there, guards and therapists alike. But, I no longer come home from work exhausted, of face the prospect of going into work knowing I will be facing hostile people.

Anger

I did, however carry with me the legacy of my prison experiences. For over a year since leaving the prison, I would have fantasies of anger. These typically occurred while I was eating in a restaurant, and would fantasize a customer taking something from my table while I was away, such as a newspaper. My fantasy was of beating the hell out of him for the theft. This is similar to a fantasy relayed to me by one of my Introduction to Psychology students, who works as a correctional officer in a local jail. He has fantasied of beating up people he talks to, such as his grandmother. In both instances, I believe the stress of the prison work, which we must mostly hold inside ourselves, wells up and demands expression. Fortunately, in my case and my student's, the expression in only via fantasy. But, it can be a good sign for protecting our emotional health, to realize that we are subject to such hostile fantasies.

Distrust

Working with prisoners had led me to have a greater level of distrust in everyday life. I now see excuses that my students present to me as likely manipulations, based on lies. This, after all, is what I typically faced from the prisoners for close to two years. Thus, I have learned to be very suspicious about anything someone tells me, especially if there is a hint of perhaps something dishonest in what the person is saying. Whereas before I might have thought that a student who says "I missed the test because I was sick" **MIGHT** by lying, now I am more likely to believe it is **PROBABLY** be a lie. My experiences with the prisoners has made me distrustful. This belief in **PROBABLY A LIE** is close to the surface. Other faculty, if asked, might say "Yes, these are probably lies" but they do not think of it so directly as I do. I had to think of it directly for almost two years in order to survive effectively in a prison. Now, that likelihood of feeling manipulated remains, even though it is no longer so important for survival.

The experiences a person undergoes will affect how that person thinks and behaves. For me to be exposed constantly to hostility and manipulation from the prisoners, or for them to have been exposed to all kinds of abuse in their early lives (see below under number 1, empathy) leads to me or them being influenced and changed (Babel, 1993; Eisenman, 1991, 1994; Gibbs, 1988; Herbert, 1994; Hoover & Juul, 1993; Lewis, 1981; Madhubuti, 1988; Paster, 1985, Patterson, 1982, Whitcomb, Goodman, Runyan, & Hoak, 1994). The exposure to hostility, aggression, or abuse cannot help but have an effect on the person, be he a young child growing up with dysfunctional parents or a psychologist working in a prison.

Two Possibly Contradictory Feelings About Criminals

I have two feelings about criminals, based on my experiences of working with them in a prison setting. On the one had, my empathy for them has increased. On the other hand, I have great hatred for criminals, much more than ever before.

1. Empathy. From working with the prisoners, I came to see that their lives had been horrible. Most had received physical, sexual, or psychological abuse, typically from their parent(s) (Eisenman, 1991, 1994). Sometimes it was from a relative or stranger. Also, most grew up in extreme poverty. Some grew up in regular, nonextreme poverty. Almost none were truly middle class. How can we condemn people from such a background, or say we would not have done the same thing (crime) if our lives had been comparably horrible? At least some sympathy seems appropriate. I came to see that these youths were, at least in part, reacting to the kinds of environments they had faced, through no fault of their own. There but for the grace of God go I. You do not have to be religious to appreciate the wisdom in that perspective. So, I now have greater understanding of how many become criminals, and this leads to a greater empathy and wish that their tragic lives can be turned around so that they will not have the rage and hatred which helps turn them into anti-social beings.

2. Hatred. On the other hand, from working with prisoners, I learned what criminals are really like. While their backgrounds may have been horrible, they, themselves are, in many ways, horrible people. They hurt others repeatedly, without remorse. Most will continue to be criminals: they will steal cars or molest children or rape or rob or whatever their preferred criminal style is. If they are in danger of being captured, or if they think they would enjoy it (perhaps influenced by drugs), they will physically attack innocent people or kill them. Thus, these youths will go on to hurt many victims in their criminal lifetime. That is why I am happy when I read in the paper that some criminal was shot and killed during the commission of a crime. I think "Good, there are numerous potential victims who will now not be hurt by this person."

My feelings here are highly emotional. True, number 1, empathy, could moderate my hatred. But, at some point, we have to realize that even is someone was abused, they must face responsibility now for their behavior and we cannot tolerate their constant anti-social, criminal conduct. To conclude that since the person was once victimized they no longer have responsibility would be to conclude that virtually no criminal could be prosecuted or imprisoned (Krauthammer, 1994).

Of course, there may be some contradiction between number 1, empathy, and number 2, hatred. But, both these feelings/thoughts exist in me, side by side. They are both the result of my working with prisoners and getting a first hand look at what criminals are like.

I was not made more or less likely to engage in crime. The criminals did not cause me to want to be more criminal, or to engage in more anti-social behavior. Nor did they did have a reverse effect on me and make me more lawabiding. Their effect seems to have been due to their daily interactions with me, which often involved them lying to me to try to manipulate me for something they wanted, be it an everyday thing such as a pass to go to the library or a more long-term gain such as a better image which would increase their chances for parole.

In conclusion, as a psychologist and therapist at the prison I tried to change these anti-social, often violent, manipulative youths. I probably had a little success, but not much since most are resistant to change. However, it is apparent that they changed me.

References

Babel, D. J. (1993). Parenting a raging child. *Journal of Emotional and Behavioral Problems*, *2* (Spring), 7.

Eisenman, R. (1991). *From crime to creativity: Psychological and social factors in deviance*. Dubuque, IA: Kendall/Hunt.

Eisenman, R. (1994). *Contemporary social issues: Drugs,crime, creativity, and education.* Ashland, OH: BookMasters.

Gibbs, J. T. (Ed.) (1988). *Young, black, and male in America: An endangered species*. Dover, MA: Auburn House.

Herbert, B. (1994, June 2). It's a tragic game of copycat. *Lake Charles American Press*, p. 4.

Hoover, J. H., & Juul, K. (1993). Bullying in Europe and the United States. *Journal of Emotional and Behavioral Problems*, *2* (Spring), 25-29.

Krauthammer, C. (1994, Feb. 7). A true test for true justice when the victim is the victimizer. *Chicago Tribune.*

Lewis, D. O (Ed.) (1981). *Vulnerabilities to delinquency.* New York: Spectrum.

Madhubuti, H. R. (1990). *Black men: Obsolete, single, and dangerous? African American families in transition.* Chicago: Third World Press.

Paster, U. S. (1985). Adapting psychotherapy for the depressed, unacculturated, acting-out black male adolescent. *Psychotherapy*, *72*, 408-417.

Patterson, G. R. (1982). *Coercive family process.* Eugene, OR: Castalia.

Whitcomb, D., Goodman, G. S., Runyan, D. K., & Hoak, S. (1994, April). The emotional effects of testifying on sexually abused children. *National Institute of Justice: Research in Brief.* (NCJ 146414). Washington, DC: U. S. Department of Justice.

Questions

1. What were the major points in this chapter? Use the rest of the page for your answer.

Questions

2. What are your opinions about the findings of this chapter? Use the rest of the page for your answer.

Chapter 4

College Student Volunteers in a Prison

College students or other volunteers are often used to work with juvenile or adult offenders (Dowel, 1978; Eskridge & Carlson, 1979; Greenberg, 1990; Kelley, Kiyak, and Blak, 1979; Kratcoski & Crittenden, 1983; Scoli & Cook, 1976; U. S. Department of Health, Education, and Welfare, 1966; Winick & Saltman, 1982). The purpose of the present paper is to present the author's observations of close to two years of how a volunteer system, using mostly college students, worked at a prison treatment program. The different kind of volunteers are described, the possible benefits considered, and some problems discussed. Some discussions of volunteers avoid discussion of problems, but others point out that problems can occur in a prison setting (Parker & LeCour, 1978) or in juvenile and adult probation agencies (Kratcoski & Crittenden, 1982).

The Different Kinds of Volunteers Observed

A volunteer may be defined as someone who provides services without pay. Following this view, there were three kinds of volunteers in the prison treatment program: (a) academic tutors, (b) companions, and (c) interns.

(a) Academic tutors came from a prestigious university located about 25 miles away, and provided academic tutoring for the prisoners, most of whom were adolescents with serious academic deficiencies. The prison was for youthful offenders, and included a school. But, the prisoners were almost all way behind in academic skills, and the academic tutors provided assistance in helping the young prisoners attempt to catch up. Thus, the academic tutors supplemented what the prison school was attempting to do. The academic tutors also served, part of the time, as companions, as it was difficult to work with these youths without becoming something of a companion. The prisoners usually welcomed contact from outside, especially from young, college-age people who were similar in age to the prisoners, but differed in being much more successful in life.

(b) Companions were specifically assigned to one prisoner with the purpose of providing companionship. The companion volunteer was instructed not to provide personal information such as where he/she worked, went to school, etc., to avoid possible future contact with the anti-social prisoners. But, they were to be friendly to the prisoners and provide a break in the routine of confinement. Companions and all other volunteers were specifically warned against trying to establish post-prison contact with the prisoners, since the staff believed the prisoners to be potentially very dangerous. Many were in for violent crimes. Thus, while they might seem nice on the outside, especially in the volunteers' once a week, one hour meeting, the prisoners were judged too dangerous by the staff to allow for possible future contact.

(c) The interns would perhaps not be thought of as volunteers by many. But, they were there without pay, often fulfilling an undergraduate class requirement. They were not the kind of interns one finds in clinical psychology Ph.D. programs, but were undergraduates learning more about the criminal justice system. Most of these interns tended to be undergraduate social work majors.

Rationale for Volunteers

Why have volunteers in the criminal justice system? One answer, and perhaps the main one, is an attempt at rehabilitation. By providing the prisoner with someone who is law-abiding and often around the same age, the prisoner is provided with a role model who is a success in life, and who does not steal or assault people. Thus, the prisoner or probationer may learn to be different by talking openly with someone who is a peer but who is very different from the kind of peers the anti-social person usually associates with (Cressy, 1955; Greenberg, 1990; Hirschi, 1969; Lemert, 1951). Also, as pointed out above, the academic tutor can provide needed academic skills, which would help the person be able to function better in society. The person who has trouble reading or doing mathematics is at a great disadvantage in getting legitimate jobs, and the criminal path will thus have appeal for many.

In addition to the rehabilitation function, volunteers also serve a humanitarian function. People who are locked up or deprived of freedom in various ways find that their life is less oppressive when someone comes and talks to them. Thus, the volunteer serves a humane function, even if they do not contribute to rehabilitation. After all, the criminal has had many years of experiences which made him a criminal. Whether brief weekly visits with volunteers will make any real difference in recidivism is debatable. But, the prisoner will suffer less while serving his time if a volunteer comes and spends time with him. This may make the prisoner a little less vicious when he gets out, or may increase the likelihood that his time in prison will be less oppressive. It may also result in decreased likelihood of assaults or riots. So, volunteers may be serving a valuable function even if recidivism rates do not change as a result of volunteerism.

Also, even if it could be shown that the volunteer did nothing to help the prisoner, the experience is of great help to the volunteer. They learn, to some extent, what criminals and prisons are like, and, in the case of interns, get to practice therapy skills, since interns were allowed to sit in on therapy groups and were sometimes, in essence, co-therapists. The volunteers in general learned about the prisoners they were working with, thus increasing their education about crime. The interns were allowed to read the case folders, thus learning a great deal about crime, the diagnosis, etc. Thus, the volunteer experience probably helped the prisoners and definitely seemed to be of benefit to the volunteers.

Problems with the Staff

The volunteer experience is not always without problems. Volunteers are outsiders, and prisons often have a negative if not paranoid-like view about outsiders. Thus, the volunteer may be seen as someone who increases the security risk, since staff have another person to watch out for, and who interrupt the normal routine (Parker & LaCout, 1978; Kratcoski & Crittenden, 1983). At the prison where I worked and observed the volunteers, I heard several complaints of how the volunteers were treated. This seemed to stem from an attitude of some staff that volunteers were a nuisance and were to follow orders and not question anything. Thus, if the volunteer drove some distance to be seeing a prisoner and that prisoner was not available for some reason (in the hospital, in seclusion) the volunteer might not be treated in a friendly fashion, but simply told, in effect, tough luck, come back next time. The prison was, in many ways, not a friendly place, perhaps due to having to control a large number of potentially violent youths. Some staff had little time for friendliness, especially to the outsiders (the volunteers).

One insight into the above problem was mentioned by a social work intern whom I supervised. He was black but said, about the staff "Even the brothers and sisters are not friendly to me. They act like I don't exist." I tried to explain to him that he was not important in their eyes, but he did not like my explanation. Nevertheless, I think it is an accurate one and accounts for his feeling of lack of friendliness, along with the general non-friendly nature of the institution.

Some of the problems volunteers had was that although the prison facility was a treatment program, many of the non-therapy staff had little understanding of treatment. In fact, some were opposed to it, and at times tried to sabotage treatment. Thus, someone coming from the outside to do what was essentially a treatment-related function, would not always be appreciated or treated with the greatest respect.

In many ways, a prison is an authoritarian institution. The people in charge are used to giving orders to prisoners and expecting immediate compliance. When prisoners do not comply, there are consequences. Thus, people who work in a prison often are used to ordering others about and expecting conformity. This proved, at times, a problem for volunteers who mostly came from academic settings which were more democratic. If the staff order was a reasonable one there might not be any problem. But, if the volunteer perceived the order as unreasonable there could be a problem. For example, one volunteer was told to help the staff pick up weights at the end of recreation. Prisoners are much into weight lifting, and weights are supplied for them. After recreation ends, the staff has to pick up and lock up the weights. In this case, the volunteer was talking with prisoners during the recreation period. When recreation ended and the prisoners were being sent back to their rooms, the staff began picking up weights. One staff member ordered the volunteer to help. The volunteer declined, believing that he was not there to pick up weights, and seeing the request as illegitimate. The staff member then ordered the volunteer to leave the area if he was not going to help with the putting up of the weights. While this example may seem trivial, out of such instances unpleasant feelings occur.

Problems with the Volunteers

At times, problems occurred because of the behavior of the volunteer. Although the rules were clearly laid out that certain kinds of personal information was not to be exchanged, some female volunteers attempted what seemed to be romantic-like involvement with the prisoners. They might include overly personal things in letters to the prisoners or hints at future meetings. Since the mail was read, these letters were quickly discovered. Or, the personal talk of the volunteer with a prisoner might be overheard. Volunteers who violated the "personal rule" were terminated immediately. In one instance, a prisoner on my therapy caseload, who appears very polite, received personal letters and interest from his academic tutor. She was terminated, which was probably the right move, as this 18-year old prisoner is a potential murderer and rapist. He has fantasies of doing both. The strange phenomenon of falling in love with prisoners or becoming sexually involved with them does happen at prisons but is closely guarded against. Since the volunteer may be seeing only the face the prisoner puts on for her, she does not really know what the prisoner is like. Thus, a very violent prisoner may appear quite nice, and, in fact, may be nice much of the time. But, personal involvement is ill advised. Incidentally, this is not just a problem for females with male prisoners, but can include males with female prisoners, or homosexual involvement with either sex.

A second problem of the volunteer concerns reliability. I had one volunteer who was seeing a prisoner who, like most of them, had received much rejection in his life. The volunteer was a former drug user who allegedly was over her drug usage. However, she missed appointments with the prisoner, without any advance notice. Also, she admitted to him that she still did speed. Thus, she encouraged drug usage in the prisoner, instead of being a role model for law abiding behavior. And, her unannounced missed appointments were taken by the prisoner as yet another personal rejection. So, this volunteer failed in her duties both with regard to her reliability of keeping appointments and with regard to the role model function. Eventually, she quit coming at all, so termination never became an issue which had to be dealt with.

The third volunteer problem is similar to the first one discussed, but also different. The problem concerns a failure to realize how potentially dangerous the prisoners are. Coming from a college campus, it is difficult to appreciate the deprivation and viciousness that prisoners have experienced. As a result, they often become highly assaultive themselves, and can hurt people with no remorse. But, in meeting them, they hardly seem like animals. Even if the volunteer is told about the crimes committed, the prisoner still seems all right, since he is not the movie or television stereotype. Instead of an animal, the volunteers see a person who looks much like them. Thus, it is easy to say, as one volunteer did, "These are not bad kids. They just deserve a second chance." She is talking about prisoners who have hurt many people, who have had second, and third, and fourth chances, and who still keep getting rearrested and show no likelihood of stopping their criminal behavior. Thus, her statement seems naive, although one could argue that given the poverty and parental neglect and abuse which most of our prisoners experienced, they never really had a first or second chance. In any event, the prisoners are much more potentially dangerous than volunteers tend to think.

Conclusions

Volunteers can serve a useful function in working with juvenile and adult delinquents. Whether this work serves to make the criminal less likely to re-offend, or simply provides a humane interlude in an otherwise depressing life, the volunteer is doing something useful. Many college students serve as volunteers to prisoners or probationers, and this should be continued. It is important for the institution to prepare the volunteer, so that the experience is a good one. Institutions need to guard against thc "us-against-them" mentality which makes them paranoid about all outsiders. Also, institutions need to see that volunteers are treated with respect and seen as someone who is there to help the goals of the institution. Then, perhaps, some of the problems discussed above would not occur. For their part, volunteers need to be reliable, law-abiding people, who keep their appointments, do not violate the rules of the institution, and serve as role models to the prisoners. Volunteers can be friendly to the prisoners without really becoming a friend, or expecting to see the prisoner outside the institution. The volunteer experience can be very educational for the volunteer and may serve an important rehabilitation function for the prisoner.

References

Cressey, D. (1955). Changing criminals: The application of the theory of differential association. *American Journal of Sociology, 61*, 116-120.

Dowel, D. (1978). Volunteers in probation: A research note on evaluation. *Journal of Criminal Justice*, *6,* 357-361.

Eskridge, C. W., & Carlson, E. W. (1979). The use of volunteers in probation: A national synthesis. *Journal of Offender Counseling,Services and Rehabilitation*, *4*, 175-189.

Greenberg, N. (1990). How college students can help delinquents. *Journal of Criminal Justice*, *18*, 55-63.

Hirschi, T. (1969). *Causes of Delinquency.* Berkeley, CA: University of California Press.

Kelley, T. M., Kiyak, H. A., & Blak, R. A. (1979). The effectiveness of college student companion therapists with predelinquent youth. *Journal of Police Science and Administration*, *7*, 186-195.

Kratcoski, P. C., & Crittenden, S. (1983). Criminal justice volunteerism: A comparison of adult and juvenile agency volunteers. *Journal of Offender Counseling, Services and Rehabilitation*, *7*, 5-14.

Lemert, E. (1951). *Social pathology: A systematic approach to the theory of sociopathic behavior.* New York: McGraw-Hill.

Parker, J. B., & LeCour, J. A. (1978). Common sense in correctional volunteerism in the institution. *Federal Probation, 32*, 43-48.

Scoli, F. P., & Cook, D. D. (1976). How effective are volunteers? *Crime and Delinquency*, 22, 192-200.

U. S. Department of Health, Education and Welfare (1966). *Preliminary research study report on volunteers in corrections.* Washington, DC: U. S. Government Printing Office.

Winick, C., & Saltman, E. B. (1983). A successful program utilizing labor union volunteers with young adult probationers. *Journal of Offender Counseling, Services and Rehabilitation, 7,* 15-26.

Questions

1. What were the major points in this chapter? Use the rest of the page for your answer.

Questions

2. What are your opinions about the findings of this chapter? Use the rest of the page for your answer.

Chapter 5

Attitudes Toward Mike Tyson's Guilt or Innocence for Rape: A Study of Southern University Students

In an earlier study (Eisenman, 1993), students at a Southern university had little sympathy for the claims of Professor Anita Hill that she was sexually harassed by Judge Clarence Thomas. Even many of the female students were vociferous in their belief that Professor Hill lied. Both males and females were especially skeptical of her charges because she waited 10 years to make them. Attitudes do not spring anew for each event. They may come from cognitive structures which give direction for a host of events which are perceived of as similar. Thus, we can often predict what someone will think about event 2 by knowing what they think about event 1, if 1 and 2 share some kind of similarity. Thus, an attitude may serve as a heuristic, guiding the person in what they perceive about a future event (Aronson, 1992; Pratkanis, 1988, 1989; Pratkanis & Greenwald, 1989).

Eisenman (1993) believed that the attitudes toward Professor Hill and Judge Thomas reflected Southern culture, especially beliefs about women and their proper role. If that is the case, then students at the same university should tend to favor the view that Mike Tyson is innocent of the rape charges for which he was recently convicted and sentenced to six years in prison. On the other hand, if the findings of Eisenman (1993) are not based on unique regional views, then the students questioned about Tyson's guilt might be split 50-50, or perhaps even inclined to be biased in the direction of thinking him guilty, since he has already been tried and convicted.

Unique aspects of Southern culture (DeLatte, 1993; Wall, 1993) and attitudes toward women (Bartling & Eisenman, 1993; Dillman, 1988) may influence subjects to believe the man instead of the woman, and thus see Tyson as innocent.

Method

Subjects

The participants were 51 students in an introduction to psychology class at a state university in the Southern region of the United States.

Procedure

During their class, the instructor mentioned that Mike Tyson had been convicted of rape and sentenced to six years in prison. He next said he wanted to see whether class members thought Tyson was guilty or innocent. He asked for a show of hands, first for the students who thought Tyson was guilty, and next for those who thought Tyson was innocent. This procedure is similar to the one used by Eisenman (1993) for the Hill versus Thomas study. It was decided, in advance, to use in the data analysis only those students who expressed an opinion. Thus, 28 students who did not indicate guilty or innocent are not counted in the statistical analysis.

A week later the class was shown the cable television movie "Mike Tyson: The Movie," and again asked for a show of hands regarding their belief about Tyson's guilt or innocence. Since the movie shows Tyson growing up as a juvenile delinquent and possibly having negative views toward women, it was thought that it might induce students to see Tyson as guilty of raping the beauty pageant contestant.

Results

The results are analyzed by a two-tailed binomial test, doubling the probabilities in Siegel's (1956) table, because he reports one-tailed results.

For the 23 students who expressed an opinion, 21 indicated that they considered Tyson innocent, and only 2 indicated that they considered Tyson guilty ($p < .002$). The two who considered Tyson guilty were both white females, but they were many more female students, white and black, who considered him guilty.

A week later, the students were shown the cable television program "Mike Tyson: The Movie," which showed him growing up in a rough section of New York City, being sent to a juvenile detention facility for his early criminal conduct, and, generally, tracing the influences on his life. The film also dealt with the rape case. After seeing the film, a show of hands revealed that 17 students still considered him innocent, and 8 considered him guilty. The ones who considered him guilty were all white females. Thus, the film had a slight effect in changing the attitudes of a few students, toward believing Tyson to be guilty of rape.

Discussion

The results are consistent with the findings in Eisenman (1993). In both studies, students at a Southern state university sided with the man over the woman: with Judge Thomas over Professor Hill in Eisenman (1993), and with Mike Tyson over his female accuser for the rape charges in the present study. It is believed that the results reflect Southern traditional values, in which men have greater status than women, and with women condemned to stay in their place, much as blacks were previously treated. If this interpretation is correct, it is interesting that women are just as likely as men to condemn Professor Hill (Eisenman, 1993) or to believe that Tyson was innocent of rape (present study). However, other interpretations are possible, and it would be desirable to see similar studies done in other regions of the United States. Perhaps these type findings would also occur in other parts of the nation.

In discussion, the reasons students gave for not believing Tyson's accuser included the following: she is a beauty contestant/model and knows how things operate, and thus would not have gone to his room at 3 A. M. unless she wanted sex; she is after publicity and money; any women who goes to a man's room at 3 in the morning is consenting to sex, or at least appearing to; and her panties and other clothing were not torn, indicating the absence of force. These statements are not presented as facts, but as the reasons the students mentioned during discussion. It would be possible to do studies using some or all of them in scripts, in which different aspects are present or absent, to see which are likely to influence perception of rape versus no rape.

With the exception of three students in the class from foreign countries (Lebanon, Denmark, and Ecuador), almost all of the students were from the state where the university is located. Thus, the sample was truly composed of Southerners, with only a few exceptions. But, until studies are done in other regions, it is currently speculation that the Southern regional nature of the students explains a great deal about their choices. Also, there may be correlated variables are important. These students tend to be highly religious, so the attitudes found here and in Eisenman (1993) might reflect conservative religious values as well as, or more than, regional influences. Often, several variables are mixed together: here the students are both Southern and conservative in religious belief.

Future studies could disentangle the relevant variables. Also, future studies could use different methods, such as having students write down their answers, and control for possible order effects. Finally, while nonresponse is often a problem if the number is too high, the fact that most students did not give an opinion in the present study is seen as not obviously a problem. Students at this university, like many students throughout the nation, are not known for closely following current events. It is desirable to have only those who truly have an opinion giving their guilt versus innocence judgments. On the other hand, the fact that only 23 students made judgments and 28 did not limits the generalizability. We can only conclude that of those who reported judgments, most thought that Tyson was innocent of rape. Blacks thought Tyson innocent.

Perhaps Tyson is such a hero to blacks that they are unlikely to condemn him or see him in a negative light.

Follow-up Study

In a follow-up study with a new sample (Eisenman, 1994), students wrote down their judgments about Tyson's guilt or innocence, instead of raising hands. A week later the same film was shown. The results were very similar. Of the 110 college students (at the same university) 80 thought Tyson guilty and only 20 said innocent, and 10 had no opinion. After seeing the film, the only ones who changed from judgments of innocent to guilty were 25 white women. All male students and all 15 black students (10 women and 5 men) continued to see Tyson as innocent. Thus, the follow-up study supported the findings of the study reported here.

In both studies, blacks were unwilling to report that Tyson was guilty of rape. All blacks who had an opinion said he was innocent. As a black hero, Tyson may have immunity with many blacks from being seen in a negative light. Perhaps if blacks had more heroes in American society, a black who is said to have offended in some way would more likely be condemned by black people. But, with few heroes and much suffering, blacks may have a tendency to feel something like "We have to stick together, against a hostile society." This explanation for the present results would fit with the behavior of some black jurors who are biased toward acquitting black defendants. In one instance that I heard of, a black female juror voted to acquit a black male defendant and later said "I am not going to vote to send another brother to prison." If blacks had more heroes and felt less hostility from society, such attitudes might not be present.

References

Aronson, E. (1992). *The social animal* (6th edit.). New York: Freeman.

Bartling, C. A., & Eisenman, R. (1993). Sexual harassment proclivities in men and women. *Bulletin of the Psychonomic Society, 31*, 189-192.

DeLatte, C. (1993, March). *Anatomy of revolutions.* Paper presented at McNeese State University, Arts and Humanities Series.

Dillman, C. M. (Ed.). (1988). *Southern women.* New York: Hemisphere.

Eisenman, R. (1993). Professor Anita Hill versus Judge Clarence Thomas: The view of students at a Southern university. *Bulletin of the Psychonomic Society, 31*, 179-180.

Eisenman, R. (1994). College students say Mike Tyson innocent of rape. *Psychological Reports, 74*, 1049-1050.

Pratkanis, A. R. (1988). The attitude heuristic and selective fact identification. *British Journal of Social Psychology, 27*, 257-263.

Pratkanis, A. R. (1989). The cognitive representation of attitudes. In A. R. Pratkanis, S. J. Breckler, & A. G. Greenwald (Eds.), *Attitude structure and function* (pp. 71-89). Hillsdale, NJ: Lawrence Erlbaum.

Pratkanis, A. R., & Greenwald, A. G. (1989). A socio-cognitive model of attitude structure and function. In L. Brerkowitz (Ed.), *Advances in experimental social psychology* (Vol. 22, pp. 245-285). New York: Academic Press.

Siegel, S. (1956). *Nonparametric statistics for the behavioral sciences.* New York: McGraw-Hill.

Wall, B. H. (1993, March). *Reminiscences of a Southern historian.* Paper presented at McNeese State University, Arts and Humanities Series.

Questions

1. What were the major points in this chapter? Use the rest of the page for your answer.

Questions

2. What are your opinions about the findings of this chapter? Use the rest of the page for your answer.

Chapter 6

AIDS Education in the Schools: How Much is Being Done?

As the HIV/AIDS problem has reached pandemic proportions, states are becoming more concerned about education as a means of informing people about the dangers (Centers for Disease Control, 1989, Russell, 1991). AIDS results in death, and is often sexually transmitted. Thus, adolescent sexual behavior and knowledge are important areas worthy of understanding (Eisenman, 1991, 1994; Keeling, 1986, 1988; Roscoe & Kruger, 1990; Russell, 1991; Strunin & Higinson, 1987) as they contribute to HIV/AIDS prevention or acquisition. The state of Louisiana requires AIDS education in all public schools, and some private schools also provide such education. But, what is really being taught?

My colleagues and I wondered if the public vs. private status of the school would matter, or the urban vs. rural location, in terms of how much students are told (Denson, Voight, & Eisenman, 1993). Also, some school systems are under Act 480, local option sex education. Schools with general approval for sex education might educate more freely about AIDS or at least about sexual aspects of transmission and the need to use condoms as a preventative measure.

Finally, minorities have been at increased risk for AIDS, often due to intravenous drug usage or other unsafe sexual practices, including homosexuality (Brannon & Feist, 1991; Centers for Disease Control, 1989) . Would predominantly minority schools differ from predominantly white schools with regard to the amount of information provided about the HIV/AIDS problem?

What We Did and What We Found

This report is based on the finding of Denson, Voight, and Eisenman (1993). A one page questionnaire was sent to the principal of 217 schools, selected in a geographically stratified fashion to reflect the make-up of schools in Louisiana. For example, since about three-fourths of the schools in the state are public, that percentage was chosen for study. The same thing was done for other concerns, such as predominantly black vs. predominantly white schools, etc.

Results

The findings were rather amazing. We got back 98 usable questionnaires (45.2%; see Rosenthal & Rosnow, 1975 and Sterrick, Barnes, & Orke, 1990, for discussions of sampling). Many principals did not know what the sex education status of their school was (30%). About 65% of the schools had not adopted local option sex education, probably reflecting the conservative, religious orientation of many school districts in Louisiana. And, the overall teaching seemed to be very limited. However, schools with sex education typically taught much more about AIDS than schools without approved sex education.

What is Taught

Intravenous drug usage and AIDS was the most frequently taught subject, but this was only taught in 58% of the schools. This was followed in frequency by statistics about AIDS (56%), history of AIDS (55%), some discussion of bodily defenses against AIDS or infection (54%), and decision making and sexual transmission tied at 52%. Only 26% of the school reported that condoms were discussed, an amazing omission.

From the above, it can be seen that non-sexual areas are apparently more comfortably taught than anything having to do with sex. This is a major deficiency in trying to teach about a sexually transmitted disease.

Blacks and Whites

Another amazing finding was that while we know that blacks are at higher risk for AIDS than are whites, the predominantly black schools reported less instruction on HIV/AIDS than the predominantly white schools. Why this should be true is not obvious. Perhaps the black schools have worse teachers, less time or money for nonstandard education, more conservatism which makes discussion of AIDS taboo (except for the issue of the death penalty, blacks tend to be more conservative than whites), less concern by parents and therefore less of a push for AIDS education, less support from the state, or any number of possible reasons. What is clear is that the group which needs the education the most is not getting it. These findings are reminiscent of a study which found that schools where drugs are the most available have the least drug eduction classes, while schools where drugs are least available have the most drug education classes (Eisenman, 1993). It seems that, sometimes, those who need an intervention the most are least likely to get it.

Conclusions

It appears that, at least within the state of Louisiana, AIDS education is very limited. It is likely that at least some of these deficiencies exist in other states, as well. Things which should be taught in schools are not taught. Perhaps the teachers who are called upon to teach about the HIV/AIDS problem do not know that much themselves. Thus, it is very difficult for them to do the job correctly. Also, the general religious conservatism throughout the state, which has a large population of Catholics and fundamentalist Protestants, makes teaching about sex a difficult problem. Many parents oppose any instruction on sex, and some school districts which teach about sex do so in a very limited fashion, emphasizing abstinence (see Eisenman, 1994, for a discussion of teaching abstinence), and no doubt avoiding many of the topics which sexually active or potentially sexually active kids wish to know about. But, ignorance is not bliss. Better education is essential. AIDS is a killer disease, and to avoid teaching about crucial aspects is to condemn some students to all the consequences of not knowing about AIDS, potentially putting them and their sex partners at greater risk for infection and eventual death. The poorer instruction in the black schools also needs correction, so that all children, regardless of race, will have effective AIDS education.

References

Brannon, L., & Feist, J. (1992). *Health psychology: An introduction to behavior.* Belmont, CA: Wadsworth.

Centers for Disease Control (1989). *Report on HIV/AIDS: January-December, 1988.* Washington, DC: U. S. Government Printing Office.

Denson, D. D., Voight, R., & Eisenman, R. (1993). Factors that influence HIV/AIDS instruction in schools. *Adolescence, 28,* 309-314.

Eisenman, R. (1991). *From crime to creativity: Psychological and social factors in deviance.* Dubuque, IA: Kendall/Hunt.

Eisenman, R. (1993). Who receives drug education in our schools?: A paradox. *Journal of Drug Education, 23,* 133-136.

Eisenman, R. (1994). *Contemporary social issues: Drugs, crime, creativity, and education.* Ashland, OH: BookMasters.

Keeling, R. P. (Ed.) (1986). *AIDS on the college campus: ACHA Special Report.* Rockville, MD: American College Health Association.

Keeling, R. P. (1988). Effective response to AIDS in higher education. *The NEA Higher Education Journal, 4* (1), 5-22.

Roscoe, B., & Kruger, T. L. (1990). AIDS: Late adolescents' knowledge and its influence on sexual behavior. *Adolescence, 25,* 39-48.

Rosenthal, R., & Rosnow, R. L. (1975). *The volunteer subject.* New York: Wiley.

Russell, C. H. (1991). *AIDS in America.* New York: Springer-Verlag.

Sterick, R. A., Barnes, J. H., III, & Orke, S. G. (1990). Comparing survey results of volunteer and randomly-selected subjects. *Psychological Reports*, *66*, 163-166.

Strunin, L., & Higinson, R. (1987). Acquired immunodeficiency syndrome and adolescents: Knowledge, beliefs, attitudes, and behaviors. *Pediatrics*, *79*, 825-828.

Questions

1. What were the major points in this chapter? Use the rest of the page for your answer.

Questions

2. What are your opinions about the findings of this chapter? Use the rest of the page for your answer.

Chapter 7

Creativity and Birth Order/Sex Differences in Children

by Sarah E. Boling, Judith L. Boling, and Russell Eisenman

Previous studies have suggested that while first borns may be higher in creativity among males, the finding is reversed for females, with later borns being the highest in creativity (Eisenman, 1967a, 1967b, 1968, 1970, 1987, 1991b; Eisenman & Cherry, 1970; Eisenman & Schussel, 1970; Taylor & Eisenman, 1968). The Taylor and Eisenman (1968) study is particularly instructive, for not only did the authors find that first born males but later born females preferred the greatest complexity (complexity is associated with creativity: Barron, 1963; Eisenman, 1991b), but the first born males and later born females were also most likely to check adjectives like those of independent subjects in a conformity study of Barron (1963). Thus, in addition to preferring complexity, first born males and later born females showed likelihood of independence of judgment,which should also be consistent with creativity (Barron, 1963; Davis, 1992; Eisenman, 1991b). However, none of the above-mentioned studies have been done with children. Thus, the present study was designed to look at birth order/sex differences with a sample of children ages 10-14, in grades 5-8.

Method

Subjects

The participants were 40 children enrolled in a grades 5-8 in a private school located in southwest Louisiana. The children were ages 10-14. There were 22 females and 18 males.

Procedure

With the permission of the school and parents, the first and third authors administered three creativity measures during a class period. These measures were: Eisenman's (1969, 1991b) Personal Opinion Survey, a 30-item, true-false, paper-and-pencil measure, which measures creativity attitudes; the 12 polygons used extensively by Eisenman (1991b) which vary from 4 to 24 points each, and measure preference for complexity-simplicity, with complexity defined by the number of points (inward points as well as outward, sticking out points); and, an unusual uses test, in which students were asked to name all the uses they could think of for a brick. This is a standard test often used in creativity research. Students were given a combined score based on number of uses (fluency) and originality of uses (originality). Originality occurs when a response happens with low frequency, typically, as in this study, when it appears less than 1% of time in the sample. The Eisenman (1969, 1991b) Personal Opinion Survey was modified slightly for this sample by the first author, taking out terms which the young students were expected not to understand. For complexity score, the students circled the three most preferred shapes on a photocopy containing the 12 polygons.

Results

Table 1 summarizes the results. An overall creativity score was obtained by combining the scores for all three tests. Since their scores were similar to the first borns of their gender, the 3 only child males and the 4 only child females were counted as first borns for statistical purposes. For males, the creativity score of first borns was

Table 1

Mean Scores, By Birth Order and Sex, on Three Creativity Measures: Personal Opinion Survey, Complexity-Simplicity, and Unusual Uses, and Combined Score.

Birth Order and Sex Group	Personal Opinion Survey	Complexity-Simplicity	Unusual Uses	Combined Mean
First born male	20.60	54.00	6.66	27.06
First born female	18.38	54.00	6.38	26.25
Later born male	17.44	35.20	9.80	20.81
Later born female	17.40	46.40	13.20	25.66
Only child male	20.00	43.33	5.66	22.99
Only child female	16.25	39.00	7.00	20.88

higher than that of later born males ($t = 1.9705, p = .0339$, one-tailed test). For females, the creativity scores of the later borns was higher than that for the first borns ($t = 1.6992, p = .0527$, one-tailed test). Both of these findings fit with expectations about birth order/sex differences in creativity.

Other findings, based on birth order alone (without considering gender) or gender alone (without considering birth order), were not statistically significant. Comparing first borns to later borns regardless of gender resulted in a t of 0.3136, $p = .75536$ (two-tailed test). Comparing males to females resulted in a t of 0.7828, $p=.4460$ (two-tailed test).

Discussion

The results were consistent with expectations based on research on college students and adults: the highest creativity test scores are obtained by first born males and by later born females. Later born males and first born females scored low in creativity. Why should these findings occur? According to the theoretical views of Eisenman (1991a,1992, 1994, 1995, in press), it may be that first born males receive greater intellectual stimulation in their family and this, along with other factors, predisposes them to be high in achievement and creativity. Why would this not hold for first born females as well?

According to Eisenman (1991a,1992, 1994, in press), the first born female receives a "double whammy" by virtue of her birth order and gender. The reasoning is that parents tend to be most restrictive toward their first child, due to anxiety and not knowing how to deal with a new baby, and toward females in general, who receive harsher socialization than males in most, if not all, societies. Thus, the first born female not only has the greater parental anxiety and restrictiveness to put up with due to being a first born, but also has a second dose of this due to being female. This is thought to inhibit creativity in first born females, perhaps because it leads them to adopt conventional attitudes inconsistent with the risk taking and nonconventional thinking need for creativity (Eisenman, 1995). The first born male would also be inhibited somewhat by the overly strong parental concern, but overcomes this as far as creativity is concerned, perhaps due to the greater intellectual emphasis the first born male gets, as a child having only adult companionship in the family, until the birth of the second child.

Other views are possible on sex differences in creativity (Eisenman, 1995; Helson, 1967) or how birth order determines personality and attitudes (Davis, 1992; Feist, 1990; Greenberg, Guerion, Lashen, Mayer, & Piskowski, 1963; Runco & Bahleda, 1987). Also, a larger sample than the one used in the present study might allow for discovery of additional findings. When subjects are put into subcategories such as birth order, sex, etc., a large sample is helpful. In the present study the findings occurred with use of a one-tailed test and at a borderline level for females. However, the present study extends our knowledge by showing once again that first born males and later born females scored highest in creativity, and this time in a sample of children, as opposed to previous studies with college students or adults.

References

Barron, F. (1963). *Creativity and psychological health.* Princeton, NJ: Van Nostrand.

Davis, G. A. *Creativity is forever* (3rd edit.). Dubuque, IA: Kendall/Hunt.

Eisenman, R. (1967a). Birth order and sex differences in aesthetic preference for complexity-simplicity. *Journal of General Psychology*, *77*, 121-126.

Eisenman, R. (1967b). Complexity-simplicity: II. Birth order and sex differences. *Psychonomic Science*, *8*, 171-172.

Eisenman, R. (1968). Personality and demography in complexity-simplicity. *Journal of Consulting and Clinical Psychology*, *32*, 140-143.

Eisenman, R. (1969). Components of creativity, verbal conditioning, and risk taking. *Perceptual and Motor Skills*, *69*, 687-700.

Eisenman, R. (1970). Birth order, sex, self-esteem, and prejudice against the physically disabled. *Journal of Psychology*, *75*, 147-155.

Eisenman, R. (1987). Creativity, birth order, and risk taking. *Bulletin of the Psychonomic Society*, *25*, 87-88.

Eisenman, R. (1991a). Birth order and development. In T. Husen & T. N. Postlethwaite (Eds.), *The international encyclopedia of education: Research and studies, Supplementary volume 2* (pp. 42-44). New York & Oxford: Pergamon Press.

Eisenman, R. (1991b). *From crime to creativity: Psychological and social factors in deviance*. Dubuque, IA: Kendall/Hunt.

Eisenman, R. (1994). Birth order and personality. In *Magill's Survey of Social Science: Psychology* (pp. 436-440). Pasadena, CA: Salem Press.

Eisenman, R. (1995). *Contemporary social issues: Drugs, crime, creativity and education.* Ashland, OH: BookMasters.

Eisenman, R. (in press). Birth order, effect on personality and behavior. In V. S. Ramachandran (Ed.) *Encyclopedia of human behavior.* San Diego, CA: Academic Press.

Eisenman, R., & Cherry, H. O. (1970). Creativity, authoritarianism, and birth order. *Journal of Social Psychology, 80*, 233-235.

Eisenman, R., & Schussel, N. R. (1970). Creativity, birth order, and preference for symmetry. *Journal of Consulting and Clinical Psychology, 34*, 275-280.

Feist, J. (1990). *Theories of personality* (2nd edit.). Ft. Worth, TX: Holt, Rinehart, & Winston.

Greenberg, H., Guerino, R., Lashen, M., Mayer, D., & Piskowski, D. (1963). Order of birth as a determinant of personality and attitudinal characteristics. *Journal of Social Psychology, 60*, 221-230.

Helson, R. (1967). Sex differences in creative style. *Journal of Personality, 38*, 214-233.

Runco, M. A., & Bahleda, M. D. (1987). Birth order and divergent thinking. *Journal of Genetic Psychology, 148*, 119-125.

Taylor, R. E., & Eisenman, R. (1968). Birth order and sex differences in complexity-simplicity, color-form preference and personality. *Journal of Projective Techniques & Personality Assessment, 32*, 383-387.

Questions

1. What were the major points in this chapter? Use the rest of the page for your answer.

Questions

2. What are your opinions about the findings of this chapter? Use the rest of the page for your answer.

Chapter 8

From Creative, Deviant Movements to Conventional Oppressor: A Look at Psychoanalysis and Women's Liberation/Feminism

As a clinical psychologist who has done psychotherapy, I look to help clients achieve growth. This often involves overcoming the old, inhibited ways of doing things, and coming up with new, original (at least for the client) approaches. An exception to being less inhibited is criminals, who often need to be more inhibited (Eisenman, 1991a, 1991b). Social movements are like clients in some ways, and what is interesting is that social movements that were once creative often become stale and oppressive. Thus, the movement was for change and reform, but eventually becomes part of the repressive establishment. I recall a politician who said about the reform group that ousted him "They said we were crooks, and that it was time for a change. Now they are as big a crooks as we were." I see two movements that started out as creative, innovative approaches, and which now show some signs of being less creative and more repressive. Creativity may be defined as originality plus usefulness. I believe a discussion of this change from creativity to repressiveness is instructive, in that deviant (nonconforming; see Eisenman, 1991a) behavior may change and become repressively nondeviant, and possibly even worse than what the movement was trying to correct (e. g., the excesses of the French Revolution: "Off with their heads."). I discuss two important social movements, psychoanalysis and women's liberation/feminism as examples. It is worthwhile to analyze social movements, both to understand them better and for implications which the analysis may have for the behavior of individuals, who also often fear freedom and retreat from it.

Psychoanalysis

Psychoanalysis may have been creative at one time, but has become less creative, at least to an extent. Part of this is no doubt due to flaws inherent in psychoanalytic assumptions (Eysenck, 1992), while part seems due to the general phenomenon discussed here of movements diminishing in creativity and tolerance.

Freud's invention of psychoanalysis was a major accomplishment. Growing up in the Victorian era, when people thought that behavior was rationally governed, Freud advanced the idea that motivation is primarily unconscious, often due to dark urges of sex and aggression. Freud was, therefore, an anti-rationalist, not in the sense that he did not use reason, but in the sense that he said reason does not form the major basis of human behavior. From Freud's ideas grew a theory; a new kind of psychotherapy (psychoanalysis); and a method of investigation, such as dream analysis and free association. Freud was no doubt wrong on many of his ideas, but his new kind of thinking was liberating, from seeing that sex was more important that people gave it credit for to seeing that people may have hidden motives in everyday behaviors, such as in the telling of a joke. For example, the joke may reveal hostility which the person could not otherwise express. Also, I believe that he was right to say that symbols, especially in dreams, are important and this was another important advance. However, his belief in universal symbols (symbol X always means Y) seems to me to be incorrect.

Freud helped overcome some of the Victorian repressiveness with his new ideas. Much of what he thought has been incorporated into our culture, so that laymen are Freudians, even if they do not know it. The Freudian ideas permeate everything from mass culture to serious writing, and most people who have not studied psychology know no other approach. Even professional advertisers know many of Freud's ideas, assume they are true, and try to incorporate them into the advertisements they produce. Thus, a product may be depicted in such a way as to appear upright and be a phallic symbol, or round and be a vagina symbol. Whether or not people truly see these things as symbols and thus are influenced to buy them is another issue. But, at least many advertisers believe they do, and create advertisements based on Freudian symbolism.

This once liberating, anti-Victorian ideology is, however, often used for repressive purposes. Here are some of the things I have actually heard psychoanalysts saying, based on their theory.

1. A man has several sexual partners. This, they often conclude, shows repressed homosexuality, and is thus, by definition, deviant in the negative sense of "deviant" (Eisenman, 1991a). The psychoanalytic concept here is that the man is engaged in a homosexual panic, defined as realizing, at some level, that he has homosexual tendencies. This induces a panic because he is opposed to homosexuality, so he engages in frequent heterosexual behaviors, with many partners, to reassure himself that he is not a homosexual. I once saw an example of this in a patient in a state mental hospital where I did my psychology internship. But, psychoanalysts, and those who follow the doctrine, make the mistake of applying, what is probably something like a one in a thousand occurrence, across the board to all men.

2. A woman is capable of multiple orgasms. We now know this to be a physiological reality. Whereas a man, after orgasm, undergoes a period of time known was the refractory stage, wherein he cannot become sexually aroused, a woman is capable of continual sexual arousal, and thus continual orgasms. Let us say that the woman induces multiple orgasms by allowing the water from the faucet of her tub to fall onto her clitoris and vaginal area. This shows penis envy, according to what some psychoanalysts have said, and indicates there is something wrong with her. Again, the person who is different in any way is put down as disturbed, even though in this example the person is functioning in what is a physiologically normal way, to give herself pleasure.

3. Students protest the policies of their university administration. According to some psychoanalysts, these students have failed to resolve the Oedipus complex adequately. The university is the father, and they are rebelling against it because they unconsciously want to overthrow their father and sexually possess their mother. This far-fetched analysis fails to consider that there may be policies which are harmful and are worth protesting against. Is all protest to be explained in terms of some unconscious problem? This is reductionism at its worst: reducing whatever is observed to some other process, in this instance a negative one. So, there is a built in conservatism to this kind of psychoanalytic doctrine. Anyone who works to achieve change is condemned.

4. A person strongly disagrees with a psychoanalyst about something. The analyst concludes that the strength of the disagreement shows that the person truly (though perhaps unconsciously) agrees, and is threatened by what the psychoanalyst has said. In this instance, you either agree with the psychoanalyst or your disagreement will be interpreted to his benefit. Either way, his position is unassailable, under the rules he has constructed.

5. A woman has sex with more than one man, and is said by the psychoanalyst to be engaging in sexual acting out. "Sexual acting out" is a somewhat vague concept, as I have pointed out (Eisenman, 1987b, 1994), but it tends to refer to the person dealing with a problem by not facing that problem, but by engaging in sexual behavior instead. I found that the concept was applied more to women than to men, which is in accord with our sexual double standard which prohibits behaviors in women which are allowable for men (Eisenman, 1987b, 1991a, 1994). This cultural standard has its effects, since females, on the average, engage in less sexual behavior than do males (Eisenman, 1982), no doubt in part because society makes them feel like they are bad if they do certain things which are, however, not prohibited, or less prohibited for males (Eisenman, 1991a).

The above examples all show psychoanalysis at its worse. One might defend the movement by saying that everyone makes errors, and that these are just some negative examples. But, the issue is, how likely are these kind of errors? I think they are very frequent, and show that psychoanalysis, at least as practiced by real-life psychoanalysts, often has a repressive, anti-creativity spirit. Instead of allowing the person to grow, the person is put into some category which serves a repressive function. The person is labeled as some kind of deviant, in the bad sense of the word (which is, unfortunately, how most people think of "deviance"), and their behavior is thus explained away as being based on some underlying pathology. Eysenck (1992) has shown that many of the assumptions of psychoanalysis are flawed and its conclusions can be better explained by other interpretations.

Women's Liberation/Feminism

Originally, the feminist movement was called women's liberation. The name change is very interesting. "Women's liberation" was a radical movement, suggesting major changes in the way women are viewed and live their lives. In 1972-73, I was a visiting associate professor at the University of California at Santa Cruz. The woman's liberation movement, sometimes also referred to as feminism back then, was a powerful, creative movement which suggested that women were being kept down in their role as housewives, and that life should entail more than taking care of a house and raising children. Women should have equality in the workplace, in the bedroom, and in general. Sexual freedom was a major part of the women's movement as I observed it then, and women opposed the game-playing which goes on in male-female relationships. Sex roles can, of course, be very confining (Cyrus, 1993). Proponents of the movement said that women's liberation would liberate men, too, and this seemed like an accurate statement. Greater sexual freedom for women and less conventional role playing would mean greater freedom for men. To demonstrate their freedom, many women's liberation advocates in California would go topless at rock music concerts, showing their freedom from oppressive rules and laws.

In later years, the term "women's liberation" was heard less and less, and was replaced by "feminism." It is less clear what feminism means per se. "Liberation" implies a radical change, while "feminism" seems to imply less. "Feminism" seems to imply the rights of women, without suggesting any need to be liberated from conventional standards.

Emphasis on Pornography and Sexual Harassment

Pornography

In recent times, not only have many feminists seemed to drop their interest in liberation and sexual freedom, but they have become sexually repressive. Two major examples are (1) the feminist condemnation of pornography and the attempt to show that it is a major cause of rape, and (2) the feminist emphasis on sexual harassment.

With regard to the pornography issue, the feminists seem to be thinking in shallow terms. Rapists are not primarily motivated by pornography, if at all. There may be individual case histories where rapists read pornography before committing a crime, but that does not mean that if there had been no pornography there would be no rape. Just because something follows something else, we cannot attribute the basis of the second thing to the first thing. If we do, we are committing the logical fallacy of post hoc, ergo propter hoc. In fact, from working with rapists and reading the research literature, many rapists come from repressive, harsh backgrounds where learning about sex, or reading about it, or looking at pictures is taboo. The best research on this was the comprehensive investigation by the Committee on Obscenity and Pornography (1970), which had vast resources, and concluded that pornography had little or no effect on behavior. In fact, one study by the commission found that rapists reported less exposure in their youth to pornography than nonrapists. While we have to exercise caution due to the self-report nature of the data, they are certainly not consistent with the feminist association of pornography with rape, and, in fact, are in the opposite direction.

Also, the issue of what is pornography is vague. Feminists usually include the relatively sanitized nudity of Playboy magazine within their definition of pornography, which is dubious. Gloria Steinem, a major feminist leader (with whom I usually agree), said that pornography is bad, but that erotica is good. The trouble is, without a clear definition, pornography is the erotica she does not like, and erotica is the pornography she does like. American society is more puritanical and sexually repressed than many think (Eisenman, 1991a). Many countries around the world have less taboos than we do about the naked body. A case could be made that we would be a more healthy society if we may had more freedom regarding nudity and sexually explicit material. In the Scandinavian countries, legalizing pornography has been associated with less child abuse, not more. I might exclude from this position pornography which combines female nudity with violence. This combination, which links in one's mind female sexuality and violence, may be harmful, while I believe most other pornography to be mostly benign. The whole idea that nudity or sexuality is bad is part of American values which needs to be overcome so that people would be liberated. If this were the case, then what we call pornography (including Playboy) would be no big deal, and would merely be seen as just another form of entertainment. Instead, today, with all our sexual inhibitions, we see pornography (or erotica; I use the terms interchangably because I doubt that they can be differentiated) as Satanic.

Sexual Harassment

Instead of pursuing sexual freedom, feminists seem out to get men, and take away some of their freedom. The concept of "sexual harassment" has been a way to prosecute and persecute men who fail to conform to some conservative standard of sexual behavior. Of course, it is important to note that true sexual harassment is horrible and has a devastating effect on the victims. But, feminists have cast their nets very wide, so that telling a dirty joke or having pin up pictures on one's wall is seen as sexual harassment. Women claim they want men to be more honest and open, but if a man is honest with a women about his sexual interest in her, he leaves himself open for an accusation of sexual harassment, because he can be accused of making an unwanted sexual advance. Since it is often impossible to know if an advance is wanted or unwanted, this puts the man in the position of inhibiting his behavior if he wants to avoid possible charges. The result reminds me of a cartoon I once saw. A man and a woman pass each other on the street. You see what they are thinking. Each would like to approach the other, but fears being thought of negatively, so they pass by without speaking. On a network television news program, feminist Robin Morgan said that men can avoid harassing women by adhering to the following rule of thumb: "If you are not sure, don't do it." While this would certainly work to cut out offensive behavior, it would also work to eliminate any kind of risk taking or creative behavior. It is the advice of repression.

Feminists have largely won in the sexual harassment arena. Their position has become the law of the land, and it is easy to bring charges of sexual harassment and put the man on the defensive. Many organizations, fearing law suits, will side with the woman and punish the man, often with no hearing or with a kangaroo court type hearing, wherein the man is sure to be "convicted" so that the organization can say "See, we oppose sexual harassment."

At other times, though, women who bring charges are, themselves, persecuted, and the organization fails to deal with real, ongoing harassment. Rape in the military is an example of this, according to a 1992 network newsmagazine broadcast. Many female soldiers are raped by the male soldiers, but often they are not believed and further harassed by the military, if they complain.

Few people have looked at the sexual harassment of males by females. This is not what feminists want, since their movement seems designed to help women and persecute men when wrong doing is alleged. It is interesting to see the knee-jerk fashion in which many (most?) feminists side with the alleged victim (female), when she makes a complaint against an alleged perpetrator (male). The feminists, without much factual knowledge, assume that the woman is telling the truth and that the man is guilty. Our study of sexual harassment proclivities in both men and women found that the same variables which related to sexual harassment proclivities by men also related to sexual harassment proclivities by women: acceptance of traditional sex roles and belief in rape myths, and other beliefs which seem to indicate lack of empathy for others (Bartling & Eisenman, 1993). One conceptual problem is that while a female recipient of some behavior might regard it as sexual harassment, the male recipient of the same behavior would often not consider what was done to him to be sexual harassment. Thus, females object to more behaviors than males object to. In this sense, females are more conservative than males.

The assault on sexually explicit material and on male sexual behavior is an attempt to turn back the clock, and make men as inhibited as women used to be and perhaps still are. So, instead of trying to liberate themselves, feminists are, in part, trying to unliberate men. It is thus a repressive, puritanical movement.

Why the Change?

Why has all of the above occurred? I do not know, although it seems to be the way things often occur: a movement starts out creative and risk taking and ends up repressive. However, I have come across an explanation of why it occurs, and although this explanation has some disturbing implications for those who believe in equality of males and females, it does provide an answer. In addition, this largely biological approach may be true, despite many beliefs in social learning explanations. We should be open-minded, especially when a theory we do not subscribe to explains something better than our own, preferred theory. Although I often lean to a social learning explanation of things, the explanation to be discussed seems to explain better the change in the feminist movement than does social learning viewpoints.

Glenn Wilson's Sociobiology Viewpoint

This explanation is the socio-biological explanation of Wilson (1992). He says that evolution has made men and women very different. Some of the differences, which he believes to be innate are that women, relative to men, are more submissive, less skilled in spatial or mathematical skills, less risk taking, but higher in empathy, verbal skills, and social skills. Wilson believes these are biological truths, not really subject to great change by culture. Thus, from this perspective, women's liberation made a mistake in trying to achieve sexual freedom and all the other kinds of freedom for women, because women do not really want this, as it goes against their nature. So, it is no surprise that the freedom of the women's liberation movement has been toppled for the puritanical repressiveness of the feminist movement. This, in a nutshell, is the Wilson (1992) perspective on the feminist movement. In some ways I am bothered by this biological determinism and its implication that things cannot change as much as one might like. But, he does provide an explanation which explains the change from the temporary radicalism of women's liberation/feminism and to the current puritanism of feminism. In fact, it is the only explanation I know of which specifically addresses that freedom-to-repression change.

An Attempted Explanation

Is there any other explanation of the change from deviant and creative to conventional and oppressive for much of both feminism and psychoanalysis? I think at least part of the answer may be found in Goldwert's (1992) statement that all great creativity is, in part, oppositional and destructive: to create one must destroy. Perhaps movements which begin by being creative have a desire, at least eventually, not to be oppositional but to "fit in" with the rest of society. Some fitting in make sense. A person or movement totally oppositional to society is in bad shape. But, the early fervor of the creative person or movement might tend to give way to a desire for acceptance, and a loss of the vision which first led to creative insights. Also, it may be that as the early leaders age they tend to become more conservative and less challenging to the status quo. In fact, as they win power and acceptance in society, they become part of the status quo. Thus, they are now the repressive establishment. Although they have the same name as the movement which once challenged society, they are now part of the informal enforcement of society's rules and mores. They have gone from deviant and creative to becoming society's cops.

Not All Feminists Agree

Some feminists do not support the assault on pornography, the simple-minded view that it is a main cause of rape, or the constant attempt to nail men on sexual harassment charges, or to verbally put them down when they do something such as telling an off color joke. Thus, some feminists have not been taken in by what appears to be the majority part, and there is hope that things could change.

Is Biology Destiny?

Biological views tend to have the implication that things really cannot change, and that the way things are is, more or less, the way things should be. However, change is still possible. If women are truly low in risk taking, for example, then there will always be a sex difference with men, on the average, being more creative than women, since risk taking is often part of being creative (Davis, 1992; Eisenman, 1969, 1987a, 1991a; Merrifield, Guilford, Christensen, & Frick, 1961; Pankove & Kogan, 1968). On the other hand, there is still room for change within cultural standards of what gender means. For example, if women are partially non-risk takers because they are taught to avoid risks, then they can be taught to take risks, and the sex difference in creativity can be reduced. Also, a biological tendency does not necessarily mean an inevitability. Even if women have an inherent tendency, relative to men, to avoid risks, they can still learn to be more risk-taking than their inherent tendency predisposes them to be. Thus, biology is destiny only in part, if this perspective is correct.

Benefits of Feminism

The feminist movement has had a powerful effect in helping women see that their potential is much more than what they have traditionally been taught. One need only to look at the letters-to-the-editor section of women's magazines to see that even fairly simple articles, about personal growth or job opportunities for women, result in letters saying things like "I never before realized that I had options in my life. This article was an incredible, eye-opening experience." Much credit for the expanded horizons for women goes to the women's liberation/feminist movement. The movement has also helped women to be more assertive and stand up for their rights, as opposed to being overly passive and being "walked on." Both men and women can often profit from assertiveness training, and it is to the feminists' credit that they recognized the nonassertive behavior of many women and sought to correct it via assertiveness training groups. And, feminists have fought for women's rights and protection in such areas as health, treatment by the criminal justice system, etc. It is tragic that the movement now seems to be headed in a puritanical, repressive direction.

A Final Warning

People are often strongly attached to their way of thinking. Thus, psychoanalysts or feminists may see my critique as so damaging to their beliefs that they will not tolerate it, and instead see me as the enemy. In fact, one person who read this manuscript said that I was trying to say that women cannot be creative. I am not saying that, nor trying to put down women. I believe strongly in the liberation of women. I am not criticizing psychoanalysts or feminists who avoid the errors described in this paper. I am trying to critique oppressive acts of what once were creative, liberating movements.

There is the possibility that what I am criticizing represents only part of psychoanalysis or feminism, and that the majority of those who identify with these movements do not do what I critique. While I suspect that I am on target, there may be many psychoanalysts and feminists whose voices are seldom heard, but who seldom or never do the kinds of things I criticized. If that is the case, the oppressors may seem to be a more dominant part of these movements than is actually the case, perhaps due to greater media publicity for their ideas.

Any strong social/political movement tends to see itself as above criticism and react strongly to deviation from group doctrine (Eisenman, 1991a). Thus, feminists who believe the current positions on pornography causing rape and on sexual harassment may not tolerate any criticism or deviation from perceived truth. For example, when one female professor, Christina Hoff Sommers, presented a paper at the American Philosophical Association criticizing some feminist positions, she reported that "...the feminists in the audience just went crazy. They had never been criticized before." (Ridgley, 1993, p. 9; see also Sommers, in press).

It seems that both psychoanalysis and feminism began as movements which strongly criticized existing social standards, but have turned into movements which, in some ways, have become as oppressive as the things they were opposing. It would be interesting to see if this is typical of social movements, or merely true of some.

References

Bartling, C. A., & Eisenman, R. (1993). Sexual harassment proclivities in men and women. *Bulletin of the Psychonomic Society, 31*, 189-192.

Committee on Obscenity and Pornography. (1970) *Report of the Commission on Obscenity and Pornography*. Washington, DC: U. S. Government Printing Office.

Cyrus, V. (1993). *Experiencing race, class, and gender in the United States*. Mountain View, CA: Mayfield.

Davis, G. A. (1992). *Creativity is forever* (3rd edit.). Dubuque, IA: Kendall/Hunt.

Eisenman, R (1969) Components of creativity, verbal conditioning, and risk taking. *Perceptual and Motor Skills, 39*, 687-700.

Eisenman, R. (1982) Sexual behavior as related to sex fantasies and experimental manipulation of authoritarianism and creativity. *Journal of Personality and Social Psychology, 43*, 853-860.

Eisenman, R. (1987a) Creativity, birth order, and risk taking. *Bulletin of the Psychonomic Society, 25*, 87-88.

Eisenman, R. (1987b). Sexual acting out: Diagnostic category or moral judgment? *Bulletin of the Psychonomic Society, 25*, 198-200.

Eisenman, R. (1991a). *From crime to creativity: Psychological and social factors in deviance*. Dubuque, IA: Kendall/Hunt.

Eisenman, R. (1991b). Monitoring and postconfinement treatment of sex offenders: An urgent need. *Psychological Reports, 69*, 1089-1090.

Eisenman, R. (1994). *Contemporary Social Issues: Drugs, Crime, Creativity and Education*. Ashland, OH: BookMasters.

Eysenck, H. J. (1992). *The decline and fall of the Freudian empire.* Washington, DC: Scott-Townsend Publishers.

Goldwert, M. (1992). *The wounded healers: Creative illness in the pioneers of depth psychology.* Lanham, MD: University Press of America.

Merrifield, P. R., Guilford, J. P., Christensen, P. R., & Frick, J. W. (1961). Interrelationships between certain abilities and certain traits of motivation and temperament. *Journal of General Psychology, 65*, 57-74.

Pankove, E., & Kogan, N. (1968). Creative ability and risk taking in elementary school children. *Journal of Personality, 36*, 420-439.

Ridgley, S. (1993). Feminism, phallocentrism, and the fat women's caucus: An interview with feminist critic Christina Hoff Sommers. *Campus, 4* (no. 3, Spring), pp. 8-9.

Sommers, Christina Hoff (In press). *The gender war.* New York: Simon & Schuster.

Wilson, G. (1992). *The great sex divide: A study of male-female differences.* Washington, DC: Scott-Townsend.

Questions

1. What were the major points in this chapter? Use the rest of the page for your answer.

Questions

2. What are your opinions about the findings of this chapter? Use the rest of the page for your answer.